B. C. IS
ALIVE
AND WELL

by JOHNNY HART

FAWCETT GOLD MEDAL • NEW YORK

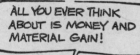

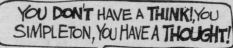

CLICK

THANK YOU

ZOW

BRUNDT

I HAVE THE ABILITY TO CLOUD MEN'S MINDS SO THAT THEY CANNOT SEE ME.

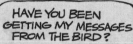

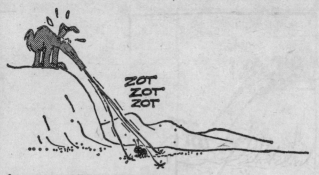

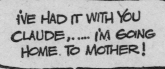

ZING

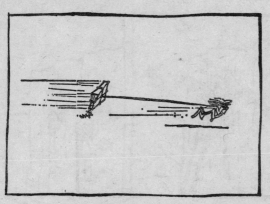

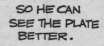

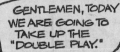

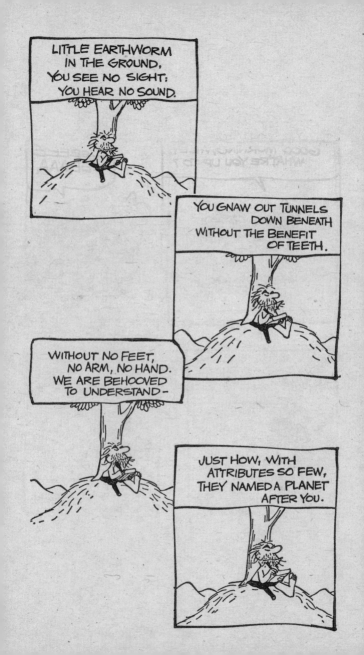

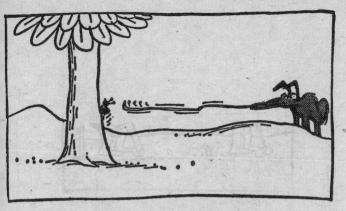

CLOMP

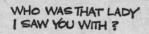

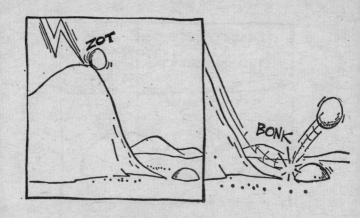

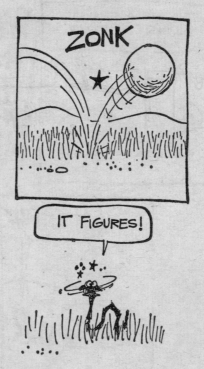

YOU WALK FUNNY.

I HAVE JUST PLANTED THE FIRST SUBTLE SEED OF INSECURITY IN MAN.